Anita J. Sullivan

THE
SEVENTH
DRAGON

THE RIDDLE OF EQUAL TEMPERAMENT

ANITA SULLIVAN

Illustrations by Sarah Bienvenu

Published by

METAMORPHOUS PRESS

P.O. Box 1712

Lake Oswego, Oregon 97034

The Western States Book Awards are a project of the Western States Arts Foundation. Corporate founders of the awards are The Xerox Foundation and B. Dalton Bookseller. Additional support is provided by the National Endowment for the Arts Literature Program.

THE SEVENTH DRAGON:
The Riddle of Equal Temperament

Sullivan, Anita T., 1942 –
    The seventh dragon.

    Includes index.
        1. Musical temperament.   2. Piano – Tuning.
3. Music – Philosophy and aesthetics.   I. Title.
ML3809.S94   1984   781'.22   84-22627
ISBN 0-943920-22-1
ISBN 0-943920-21-3 (pbk.)

Acknowledgement
    Excerpt from *"Letter on Harmony* by Regino of Prum"* tr.
by Kathi Meyer-Baer in *The Music of the Spheres and the Dance of Death*, reprinted by permission of Princeton University Press.

Typesetting and copy layout by Cy-Ann Designs, Portland, Oregon 97219
Printed in Hong Kong by Wing King Tong Co Ltd

To Sam, who chose to remain invisible.

ACKNOWLEDGEMENTS

I have many collaborators in this work, most of whom do not even know they had any part in it. The best collaboration always comes about as a result of conversation, I think, and how can you thank someone for something so freely given? Chief among those with whom I have conversed specifically about the material in this book (and with whom I continue to converse) are Sam C. Stuart, Marcia Mikulak, and Douglas Leedy — who are also Listeners. My children, Patrick and Timothy Sullivan, have been involved in the making of *The Seventh Dragon* from the beginning, and I appreciate their ideas.

THE SEVENTH DRAGON:
The Riddle of Equal Temperament

Dramatis Personae

The Seventh Dragon: referred to as "he."
The Tuner: referred to as "she."
The Piano: referred to as "it."

TABLE OF CONTENTS

Author's Preface

It may come as a surprise to you, as it did to me, to learn that the tuning of a piano is not at all the same as the tuning of a violin or a guitar. Not only is it physically more difficult (and time consuming), simply because a piano has over 200 strings, and they are "tied down" very firmly by their tuning pins — not only that: a piano is tuned by a wholly different philosophy.

The novice piano tuner is told that she must first "set a temperament" before doing anything else. This means that in the middle-C area of the piano she must tune certain intervals — chiefly fifths, fourths, and major thirds — so that each one is a little bit out of tune. *How much* out of tune is the "rule" imposed by Equal Temperament, the tuning system which has been used on pianos for about 150 years (the piano is about 250 years old). Other instruments do not need to be tuned this way. They do not begin with a temperament, which is a kind of deliberate pattern of mis-tuning administered

vii

to a small portion of the instrument, to which the whole instrument can then be adjusted; for simpler instruments the tuning *is* the pattern.

Why are pianos different? What is the philosophy behind Equal Temperament? Why do I call it a philosophy, instead of just "a tuning system"?

Therein lies a tale. Somewhere along the way between the mere four or five or even twelve or sixteen strings used on violins, lutes and other non-keyboard stringed instruments, to the couple of hundred which are stretched across the wide soundboard of a piano, a border was passed. A new dimension was entered which made the whole phenomenon of tuning something of an acoustical cauldron. And the new situation, which was really not new at all, turned out to be a painfully obvious manifestation of a riddle which had puzzled musicians, instrument builders, musical theorists, and philosophers for centuries: What is this thing we are calling music?

You would think there would be a simple, obvious way to tune a piano. Especially if tuning means bringing something into harmony. Surely if that cannot be done, then we have gravely misunderstood our universe and our purpose within it. But what is harmony? We have thought it means agreement, concord, and a feeling of serene beauty. In acoustics it means intrainment — or, musically-vibrating parts of an instrument moving together by the same rules, rather than each working under a different directive. But it turns out that Nature has many directives, or structures, available which she manifests in a multitude of forms. These structures are the patterns, or "rules," but they can reveal themselves
viii

in ways which are confusingly similar.

Like a magnet, the piano seems to have drawn from Nature more than one structure or set of rules by which it can operate. So, it turns out that when we sit down to make harmony by tuning this enormous instrument of iron and wood and seven-plus octaves, we discover it is rife with possibilities. All at once "harmony," which we thought was only one thing, becomes a matter about which decisions have to be made, and about which compromise is possible — even necessary. This shakes us. Harmony, as we know from the physics of musical acoustics and from philosophies and religions all the way back to Pythagoras (perhaps beyond), is based on numbers. And numbers are nice and stable; they just *are*. Surely, they are not subject to the whims of human judgment;

The pattern which tradition and numbers have conspired to produce on the keyboard of the piano is the diatonic scale. The tuning of a piano by the system of Equal Temperament (or by any of the myriad of other temperaments which are possible, even if rarely used on this instrument), results inevitably in some version of this scale. It is the scale of Western music; most of us have never heard any other. To the dismay of many music educators around the world, music made by this scale has displaced traditional music in the majority of non-Western countries. It was Bach's scale, Mozart's scale, and now is doing service for hard rock, pop music, and even synthesizers — those electronic marvels which some say will be the piano's eventual replacement — automatically tune themselves to the piano's Equal Temperament. Indeed, any music played on the keyboard — organ, harpsichord, synthesizer, or piano — including avant-garde contemporary pieces which use chromatic modes or jazz chords, or some atonal combination of pitches, is still being played in the diatonic scale. This situation has prevailed for over 100 years. The piano keyboard has, during a good part of its lifetime, contained the "authorized version" of this very powerful and versatile scale. Yet all the music we hear coming from the twelve tones of the piano's authorized-version octave is "made out of" fifths, fourths and thirds — those very intervals which the piano tuner has deliberately put out of tune. Is not this something we should know about?

*sotto voce: This is a voice, often more scholarly than that of the narrator, which runs as a kind of basso ostinato to the main body of the work.

Foreword

For thousands of years the art and science of music was enlivened by a running debate over what were the truest and most musical tuning systems. One might pause and reflect on some of the illustrious names that engaged in this discourse: Pythagoras and Aristoxenos, Plato, Boethius, Johannes Kepler, Vincenzo and Galileo Galilei, Christian Huyghens, Johann Joachim Quantz, Leopold Mozart; Jean-Philippe Rameau seemed to favor several different temperaments (including 12-tone equal) at different times; Telemann was an enthusiastic proponent of a theoretical 55-tone equal-temperament system; and J. S. Bach's feud over temperaments with the great instrument-builder Gottfried Silbermann is one of music history's well-known tales.

We are now, alas, deprived of such a vital (and consequential) aspect of musical life, and have been since the acceptance of 12-tone equal temperament as a universal definition of interval sizes in Western music, an acceptance that was complete by the beginning of the present century. Musical connoisseurs and amateurs alike now regard the pitches defined by that temperament as self-evident, a given fact not to be questioned. The rationale of temperament, its practical and philosophical meaning, and the science of tuning and intonation are unfortunately no longer a part of a musician's education.

For most pianists the piano is a "black box," the inner workings of which, from the escapement to the setting of a temperament, are no less mysterious than is the circuitry inside the TV set that may entertain them with "Dallas" or, for that matter, "Nova" or "Masterpiece Theatre." The modern piano is a machine-age product, and the piano-tuner must remain to a large extent one of those indispensable specialists of that age, since piano-tuning is a skill that demands a mental and physical involvement beyond the reach — and interest — of most people who own a piano.

Piano tuners probably have considerable opportunity to reflect on their craft during the lengthy and repetitive effort that goes into the tuning of a piano. Anita Sullivan's engaging reflections on the piano tuner's art have not only let us in on the intimate relationship between the tuner and the instrument with which she must commune in her craft, but have revealed to us a human face of equal temperament, a musical compromise that is thoroughly a product of human rationality.

She understands, like those of us who have done a lot of tuning, and who have spent many hours trying to find the true temperament that lies latent within an

xii

instrument, that as we tune that instrument, it is also tuning us. Beyond helping us to understand and appreciate what it is that the tuner does, her delightful book will certainly put all lovers of the piano a little bit more in tune with their instruments.

Douglas Leedy
Portland, Oregon
July 24, 1984

Douglas Leedy is a Portland composer, performer, gardener and classical philologist who has written extensively on tuning systems and intonation.

Prelude

There is a mystique about piano tuning.

"I'm going to have my piano tuned today" doesn't come out quite the same as having the rugs cleaned or taking the cat to the vet. Why not?

Maybe it has to do with the piano. Not only is it a musical instrument, but an exceptionally large one. You are aware that it contains a good deal of iron and steel in addition to wood, and thus is massive and full of tension. For these reasons alone it commands more respect than, say, a washing machine.

And there is the tuning. Even if you are accustomed to tuning your own guitar or violin or autoharp, you must call in someone else for your piano. And what does this person do? You've probably never thought much about it. Isn't tuning something a tuner "does" to a piano, like sweeping the chimney or changing the oil in the car — routine maintenance? Isn't it the same process every time?

No, it is not.

First of all, the tuner is not coming to tune a piano: she is coming to tune *this* piano.

Aside from that, there is much more. I would like to tell you about the wonderful mystery, the enigma, of tuning your piano.

xiv

"That there is music in the motion of heaven has been recognized and explained by the Pythagoreans. How is it, they said, that so fast an engine as heaven is run so quietly and silently? And though the sound does not reach our ear, it is impossible that so fast a motion does not carry a sound, especially as the course of the stars functions with such great adaptation and convenience that nothing else like it, so combined and interwoven, is within our comprehension. Because some courses are carried out higher and some lower, and, thus, all turn through the same original impetus, the order of the courses must follow different ratios. Therefore it is supposed that in the motion of heaven an order of ratios is contained. The consonance which is at the bottom of all measurement in music cannot originate in sound . . . Of the motions, some are faster and some slower; and if motion is slow and uneven, a low sound is produced, but if quicker and more intense, necessarily a high sound is produced. If a thing is not moved, no sound arises."

(Excerpt from First Chapter of *Letter on Harmony* by Regino of Prum, c. 900 A.D. Tr. by Kathi Meyer-Baer)

First Interval

"In many a forest falls a tree
That no one hears.
Not for lack of sound,
But ears."
(Anonymous)

The Seventh Dragon in Japanese folklore is the only one of nine who is never seen. All eight brothers and sisters, even his mother, are depicted in art, carrying on their individual special tasks. They grimace from beneath tables, look down from the fronts of buildings, decorate the pages of books, ornate and terrible. Why is the Seventh always absent? No one has ever explained. His special task is listening; that is how he is identified. Perhaps he never shows up because his visible self is constantly consumed in the act of hearing.

Like the Seventh Dragon, a piano tuner is a Listener. Although she does not disappear each time she leans

1

over a piano, and become invisible to the other people in the house, her task involves the imbibing of musical sound.

But what is there about sound which can render a dragon invisible?

Normally, the world that our eyes bring us is the one we notice most — the world of things. But sounds are not things, exactly. "Sound" is a catch-all word which describes "all that we hear," in one lump, from music to noise. Although that is a broad agenda to be subsumed by a single word, we consider the kingdom of our eyes far more complex, and would not dream of trying to sum it up in a word which would mean "all that we see."

When we try to understand sounds, we describe them in terms of air moving in tight little bunches. In order to comprehend what is happening inside our ears we must visualize the whole phenomenon by recording the compressions and rarefactions which the air makes, on pieces of paper. They make funny shattered, clumpy patterns which we call "graphs". Because we see these patterns, we think that we now understand the nature of sound.

Nevertheless, it is difficult to imagine Beethoven's Violin Concerto as "merely" a series of compressions and rarefactions of air molecules making their uneven way through the canals of our ears. Surely there is a translation in process, one which by-passes the blobs and waves on the graph paper. Perhaps it could be called a transfer — from the outer ear to an inner listening place.

For it is impossible to understand sound by visual-

izing it. To think of sound as a by-product of motion —
but not to restrict it to that — is some help. There is no
sound without motion (but not all motion causes sound).
The air is daily filled with thousands of intense motion
patterns, a constantly changing mosaic which we call
"click, whirr, scrape, whine, roar, just plain noise — or
music." There was a time (before the invention of the
printing press, perhaps) when ears were more important
than eyes, both for protection and to bring us informa-
tion about food, weather, and how many other creatures
were munching in our general vicinity. Our ears can
reach around corners; our eyes cannot. Before people
read, education took place largely by memorizing that
which was chanted or spoken or sung. Today, what we
hear merely accompanies or enhances what we are
looking at (would video games be interesting if they were
silent?) — our soundscape is composed of fragments.

But can we listen to sounds we are not able to hear?
Everything is moving, so physics tells us. Yet our ears
hear only in a limited range of frequencies (20 to 20,000
cycles per second). The majority of the motion going on
in the universe remains outside even that seemingly
generous range. The sun, for example, has regular
acoustic vibrations, approximately 16 minutes in frequency. What kind of a gong would fill the atmosphere
if that could be heard by our ears! The many ancient
and medieval philosophers who kept insisting the universe was making beautiful music, even though we
couldn't hear a note of it, would feel vindicated to know
that the sun, the mountains, the earth itself, all vibrate
with what we call acoustic frequencies. This means both
the nature and the range of the vibrations is considered

sonic, even though our ears may not be equipped to hear them. The frequencies may be below the threshold of hearing, as with the sun's vibes, or above it, as in ultrasonic oscillations — those made under certain conditions by whistles and magnetized rods, and quartz crystals, and dolphins. Motion patterns rain upon us all our lives, but our ears are only responsible for translating a tiny portion of them.

If you watch cellist Mstislav Rostropovitch and can take your eyes from his face long enough to see his fingers move, you might just wonder what kind of sound would come from the left hand, the one which trembles in vibrato over the strings. We do not hear that hand, though it moves constantly throughout the composition. The air around the cello has another priority — it dances to the back-and-forth of the strings, which are caught and released by the bow many hundreds of times a second. One human hand, however, even when it is moving as rapidly as it can, is almost powerless against the air's dumb inertia.

Since there are sonic vibrations which we cannot (or at least, do not) hear, is there something in the nature of these particular, unhearable, sounds which nonetheless might be rendering our Listening dragon invisible?

Invisibility might indicate that our dragon resonates to an ultrasonic frequency, and that normal sound destroys him — like the shattering of glass. Or, alternately, if we think of our dragon as being composed of harmonic, sinusoidal, wave patterns, then his invisibility might be simply a kind of silence on his part. When the nodes of musically-generated sound waves intersect, silence is the positive, if temporary, result. Perhaps our invisible Listening dragon is really an anti-dragon, particularly sensitive to musical wave patterns, and thus he only appears during those moments of silence which occur in music so rarely and so briefly they are virtually non-existent, and when there is no music playing, these moments do not occur at all. That may be why the piano tuner, who is deliberately playing with sinusoidal curves, and is tuning an instrument which now and then produces something close to a set of pure overtones, might, if she is fortunate, catch a glimpse of that grand old creature of silence, complete with wings and tail.

However, it is more likely that the dragon is invisible because he is a Listener. This has to do, not with sound, but with ears.

Could it be that we receive some of the unhearable sounds, the acoustical vibrations which are too high or too low for our ears, could it be we receive them in ways other than by hearing? Hearing, after all, is a specialized form of the sense of touch. Must the idea of sound begin and end with whatever stirs our eardrums into action?*

Listening is a capacity we hardly know we possess. It is possible to make of the body a sun, which draws sound up like water from a rain puddle. The ears only tell us what we have done, afterwards: but during the listening every cell will incline in that direction, and the entire world will rise into us like glorious, palpable, mist.

A piano tuner is a Listener, not just one who hears. Her listening is not something she does, suddenly, each time she opens the piano lid; she is doing it all the time,

*See page 6 *sotto voce.

like breathing. And the tuning, a result of listening, is not imposed upon the piano. She does not bring it forth from her tool box and say, "Sir and Madam, here is a Tuning. I will now proceed to administer it to your piano. It is the same Tuning with which I dose all pianos. That will be $40, please."

*sotto voce: It is undoubtedly true that a blind piano tuner has the advantage of all blind people who of necessity have compensated for the loss of one sense by the enlargement of the capacity of the others. Nevertheless, it is my belief, based on nothing but intuition, that a sighted piano tuner uses her eyes, as well as all her other senses, to enhance listening — not to distract from it (although that is definitely possible too, if someone has an interesting picture hanging above the piano!). When I tune, I find myself staring fixedly at the tuning pin and the strings, almost as though I were "seeing my way into" what the string is doing. I suspect that somewhere in the complex circuitry of receiving areas in the brain, there is a redundancy at work, which means the "seeing" section and the "hearing" section are not rigidly cordoned off from one another, but actually use some of the same "wires." Sometimes, I confess, I can scarcely tell the difference, when I am tuning, between the sounds I hear and the thick ambience of color and transparent air which swirls around my head.

No, if the piano has been well made, and if it has been tuned well from infancy, the tuning is already there, like a template in the very structure of the instrument. The tuner must listen until every last note of it is drawn up into her tuning hammer, into her body, into her mind and soul. Only thus, as she moves from pin to pin, waiting each time a split second before her hands move, does a tuning take form. The piano tunes itself, through the tuner. If she is pure and still, the piano's unique harmony will find its way through her, to others, who also listen.

(Conversation overheard between two tuners)

A: But some pianos are so badly made. How can you tune them well?

S: There are as many different ways of listening as there are pianos. Don't listen too hard to a spinet. It's not a quiche, it's just a pickle. But it can be a good pickle.

A: Oh, you mean, bring out the best it is capable of?

S: Something like that, yes.

A: But some pianos don't seem to know anything. They don't know how to be tuned. There is no harmony at the core when I listen, only confusion.

S: In that case, you have to listen even harder, to what that piano *should* be, and show it the way. It is not easy. Some of them put up a good fight.

Second Interval

arrest, resist, inhibit, restrain, oppose, withstand, conflict, antipathy, tension, impedance, opposite, overcome

". . . Neither from nor towards; at the still point, there the dance is, but neither arrest nor movement. And do not call it fixity, where past and future are gathered. Neither movement, from nor towards, neither ascent nor decline. Except for the point, the still point, there would be no dance, there is only the dance."

(T.S. Eliot "Burnt Norton" part II)

To help a piano make music, more than listening is required, of course. Pianos are strong and tough. Even

9

the smallest spinet is put together of several hundred
pounds of dense hardwood and heavy iron alloy. A
piano is built, among other things, to resist. It will
resist humidity, heat, drafts, paper clips and pencils
dropped inside, mice, years of neglect, sliding across a
carpet, being lifted . . . It also resists being tuned.

A piano is born in a state of high tension, much
more so than a wheelbarrow or a lamp. The piano is sent
into the world with this tension arrested. It is the task
of the tuner to re-arrest.

Each time a tuner places her hammer upon a tuning
pin and begins to turn it, she is exerting a force of 15
pounds or so.* Most of the opposition comes from the
friction of the threaded pin against the many wooden
laminations of the pin block, in which the pin is buried
about an inch and a quarter. The rest of the resistance is
provided by the steel string, with the cooperation of
everything it touches on its way from the tuning pin,
down under the pressure bar, across the open space of
the sound board, around the bearing pins on the bridge,
and over the hitch pin on the back (or at the bottom, in
an upright) of the metal plate.

In the course of a tuning, each of the 200-odd
tuning pins is urged, ever so slightly, from its slot,

*sotto voce: This exertion is properly, "foot pounds".
The amount of resistance in the exact center of the
tuning pin, in a healthy pin block, is probably about
150 to 180 pounds. But a tuning hammer is roughly a
foot long, and this leverage makes it possible to turn the
pin with about as much pressure as it would take to lift
something weighing 15 or 20 pounds.

turned a fraction of an inch, then released in its new position. The piano, meanwhile, exerts the full strength of its bulk and tension to keep the status quo.

The status quo is the maintenance of 18 to 30 tons of tension across the full length and width of the instrument. Only thus can the steel strings be tight enough to tremble at the proper musical frequencies. Only thus can they transfer their tremblings through the bridges to the resonating sound board. Only thus can that hulk of furniture in the corner of the living room emit the kind of pleasing, lovely sounds we expect from it.

If a piano were to relax, as we humans keep trying to do, it would be something else altogether. A piano is full of suppressed desires, recalcitrance, inhibition, conflict. Yet because its opposing forces are carefully balanced, they are still. And the still place, though small, is where music can spin its way through into our dimension.

The laws of entropy work on a piano, as they do on everything else. Because its state of imposed high tension is in a sense unnatural, and the stresses which its materials maintain as a matter of course are unusual, it must have its abnormal state constantly re-imposed. Left alone, the piano will slide gradually into chaos — slide, and grind, and rub and split (secretly, and slowly, as a growing plant). If the tuner never comes, and if the piano is never played, the tension which keeps it alive will gradually melt away. The piano will cease to be in arrest, and will start to move, to decline, into the cozy state of randomly drifting slow molecular motion in which abide its more humble companions (wheelbarrows and lamps. People.) At the end of the path of least resistance, for a piano, is an awful puddle of noise.

The tuner comes with the strength of her arm, to resist the piano's slide into chaos, and by opposing, postpone it. For an hour and a half or two she pulls back against the piano's relaxing tendencies, seeks to overcome its motion, to force it back into stillness. She touches many hundred of the piano's thousands of parts, which in their turn touch others, and gradually all is re-aligned. Somewhere along the way the piano ceases to lean, to resist, its confusion clears, and its great strength swells into a mighty Yes!

Tuning, then, restores the piano's natural state — a state of "unnatural" high suspension. But a piano's particular alignment is very particular indeed. It is de-signed to make certain sounds, which we recognize as familiar and beautiful. It does not continue to make these sounds of its own accord, but must be regularly tuned. What kind of sounds is a piano supposed to make? How does the tuner know when the piano's proper balance has been re-established, so that it is making these sounds? Is there any room in there for the tuner as mechanic to blossom into tuner as artist? What do we hear when the piano is in tune?

Tuner's Monologue

<u>Knowing when to stop</u> — *Tuning is constant motion. Lifting the hammer, putting it down on the next pin (wiggling a bit to make sure it settles), then the slight pull with your hand. The other hand, meanwhile, striking the piano key, over and over. Pull, push. Strike, strike. Pull, strike. Push, strike, strike.*

The note you are striking comes to the center of your head. It sketches itself onto your ear-vision as a pure color, attached to no shape, whose only quality is a shine. Your head is filled with shine-sound, which shimmers; its facet tilts; it pulses to awayness. You stop.

Immediately you begin again, on the next note. But you have left behind the last one, because you stopped. You stopped when you came upon what you were listening for. And it was not sound at all (oh, the enormity of that first discovery!), but a place in the center of all the pronged tremblings which are struck notes. All around your head. Then stop.

It is like silence would be, if we could hear it, but of course we cannot.

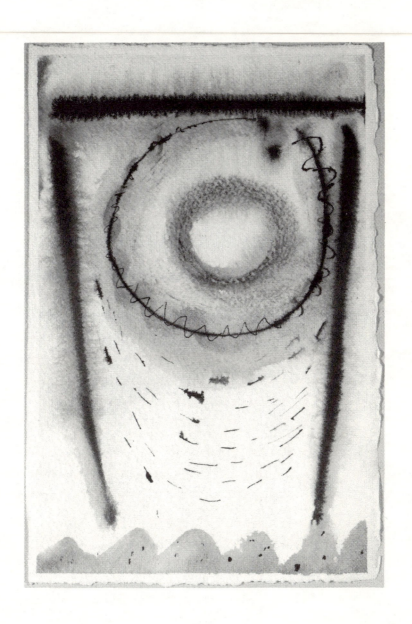

Divertimento on the Piano Keyboard

Pianos need to be tuned, then, for a physical reason. In terms of Aristotle's causality this might be called the material cause (or perhaps material and efficient together). But the reason behind that reason is really more important to us: we tune our pianos because they sound terrible if we do not. This might be called the formal cause.*

Let us take a few minutes to describe the piano keyboard, so that we will better understand why it makes the particular sounds it makes.

If you have a piano nearby, stroll over to it. Look at the keys. There are 88 of them, in a straight line, encompassing a width which most adults can comfortably span with both arms. Make a note in the back of your mind that the keyboard is straight, not curved. In fact, the playing area of most instruments (the place where you put your fingers, or your bow, mallet, etc.) is straight. Each piano key, when depressed, sounds a single note, starting with the lowest at the bottom or left side of the keyboard, and progressing up, step by step, each note higher in pitch than the one behind, to

*sotto voce: If you would like to be refreshed, Aristotle's four kinds of causes are: Material, Efficient, Formal and Final. A good discussion of the meaning of these causes occurs in David Bohm's excellent book Wholeness and The Implicate Order on page 12.

the final highest C at the top. Each note is represented inside the piano by one, two, or three strings.

We use seven letters of the alphabet to name the 88 piano keys, black and white.* Starting from the bottom note, A, each white key has a letter name, A-B-C-D-E-F-G. After that the white keys start over again with A, and so forth, right up to the top of the piano, where the last note happens to be a C. What about the black notes? Although no black note has a sound exactly like any white note, they do not rate letters of their own. Instead, the black notes are called by the same letter as the white key just to the left or right of them, with the word "sharp" or "flat" added. When the black key is thought of as above (or to the right) of a white key, it is that white key's "sharp"; when it is being referred to as lower, (or to the left), it is the white note's flat." For example, the second key on the piano, a black key, can be either "A-sharp" or "B-flat." The choice is made by the composer according to certain rules.

Each section or "clump" of white and black notes, A through G-sharp and back to A again, is called an octave. "Octave," as you probably know, means "eight," and if you count both the A at the top and bottom of the octave, and all the notes between, you certainly end

---

*sotto voce: Bear in mind throughout this book, and for that matter in other books, that whenever any formal system is being described, there are almost always other systems which could be in effect instead. The one which happens to prevail at any one time is not necessarily the best of all possible systems. The color, shape, and naming system of our piano keys is one example.

up with more than eight notes. Yet we have continued to use the word "octave" to describe the outer boundary of our diatonic scale, long after the extra notes were squeezed into it: possibly because for a long time musical tradition did not universally sanction the introduction of those extra tones, and considered them "beyond the fringe."

Each octave, then, contains seven white notes and five black ones. These twelve distinct tones are each duplicated, in a higher or lower pitch range, by the octave to either side. That is, every A on the piano sounds like itself in tone, but not in "highness" or "lowness." So also every B, C-sharp, etc. has its duplicate seven times over (sort of like echoes). The piano keyboard expanded from a harpsichord size of slightly more than four octaves, to its present range which extends from an A at the bottom, through seven full octaves, with three notes left over at the top for no significant reason.

This system limits the music we can make on the piano to twelve tones. We can play those tones at various different pitch levels, all up and down the keyboard, but there remain only twelve different possible tones with which to fashion our piano music.

Obviously there are many more than twelve possible musical sounds that can be made inside an octave. Why have we opted for the particular combination which is there on the piano? Do all pianos always sound the same twelve tones? Who made this decision of what kind and how many, and why?

Third Interval

"Art steps in when Nature fails."
(from a corset advertisement in a
19th century newspaper)

We have just finished limiting the piano to twelve tones. Those are the ones which are actually there, duplicated in each of the piano's seven-plus octaves. But if a piano can be tuned, if the tuning pins can be turned, and the strings can thereby be tightened or loosened, then a logical inference leads us to conclude that the whole piano *could* make music of a different sort. And indeed it could.

If you think about it, this places the tuner in a position of power. Like one of the nine Muses who originally was thought to spin the heavenly discs which kept the Universe singing in perfect harmony, she too must keep harmony. By tightening this string or that one, a little more or less, she regulates the pitch of each note, and

21

thus determines how the notes will sound together. Of course, if her decisions are arbitrary or indifferent, the piano will sound "out of tune," and she will soon be out of work. In practice, the tuner is restricted by physics and custom to a certain parameter. For some tuners this might seem small indeed; for others, even a unison can be a chasm.

When a piano tuner begins to tune, she starts her operation in the center of the piano. Here she performs an operation called "setting the temperament." She does not play one note at a time and compare it to a tuning fork, to determine the proper pitch; instead she plays two notes at a time — an interval — and listens for the "beats" which are made by the intersecting patterns of the vibrations of the two tones. These "beats" are a way of measuring the degree of purity or harmony which she is hearing. She carefully regulates that harmony a certain amount away from pure. When all the intervals in the center are properly balanced, she then tunes by octaves, outwards towards the bass and treble extremes of the keyboard. The result is not perfect symmetry, nor a collection of pure intervals, it is a balance — a compromise.

For the past 150 years or so, pianos have almost always been tuned by a system called "equal temperament." And though it is not the only combination of intervals which can be used to make tone relationships on a piano, we have become so accustomed to the music that this system produces that many musicians and music theory books do not even take notice of the fact that anything else is possible, on a piano or on any other instrument. How this state of affairs has come about is an interesting story, yet remains somewhat of a puzzle withal.

The place of the piano in music history has something to do with it. Although instruments with keyboards have been in use since ancient Greek times, it is only with the modern piano that the "keyboardness" in itself became a dominant element in determining what kind of music the instrument could and should play. We have ten fingers with which to manipulate the piano keys. Those fingers can move very quickly, and can come down on ten keys at once. This makes certain combinations of sounds very noticeable. Music is usually meant to "pleasure" our ears, not to insult them. And though people don't always agree upon what is beautiful in music, they do tend to notice when something disturbs them.

We did say a piano, like a harpsichord or organ or organistrum — other keyboard instruments — can be tuned by a system other than equal temperament. Early pianos, in fact, were tuned by other temperaments, for about the first 100 years of their existence. People in the past, listening to those tunings, did not then think of their pianos as "out of tune." But we would think so. Listening to a piano tuned in a "meantone" temperament, or an "irregular" temperament, we would wince.

Likewise, if a Medieval or Renaissance citizen were to appear suddenly tonight in the audience during the performance of Beethoven's Emperor Concerto, his first reaction would probably be to cover his ears. The loudness and clarity would overwhelm him before he had a chance to notice the balance of the chords. In an historical sense, this is exactly what the piano did to the collective ears of many generations. Their response created a need — not for quiet (the trend has been away from that for a long time!) but for harmony.

Do we, then, have harmony on our pianos, tuned for the past 150 years in equal temperament? Not exactly. We have compromised. The particular compromise we have chosen, equal temperament, is only one of many which we could have chosen instead. Why compromise is necessary, and why we have opted for equal tempera-ment, are questions which force us to keep looking back and forth between what we *want* from music, and what it is possible to make a scale system *do* on an instrument.

Tuner's Monologue

<u>Hand and ear</u> — Hands are so inexact. If my ear could do the tuning we would have been done before this. But the hand is not small enough, here. (Here where sound is so thin it could not be seen if it were turned into a thread.) Weaving these invisible threads of sound is difficult with a two-pound lever of wood and steel, held in my hand. I lean on the hammer, just as a skater leans into the wind. The pin must not turn far — it is coaxed into a shred of a circle. My will moved it, surely, not this hand.

Fourth Interval

perfect   imperfect

rational   irrational

purity   impurity

regular   irregular

equal   unequal

symmetrical   asymmetrical

order   chaos

pattern   chaos

harmony   discord

equal   proportional

uniform   proportional

uniform   pattern

pattern — pattern

random

order   order

pattern   uniform

proportional   uniform

proportional   equal

discord   harmony

chaos   pattern

chaos   order

asymmetrical   symmetrical

unequal   equal

irregular   regular

impurity   purity

irrational   rational

imperfect   perfect

29

If a piano tuning represents a compromise, what is the nature of the extremes? What do we relinquish in this equal temperament system that we might just possibly prefer, if we could retain it? Do we have a right to be disgruntled?

The idea of compromise in natural forces occurs in other areas than music. It usually happens because we want many things to work together, and only a few will do so perfectly. The most familiar example, probably, is the efforts to combine the natural periodic rotation systems of Earth around the sun, and moon around the Earth. Although the sun system has won out in our 365-day calendar, the twelve months are a tribute to age-long efforts to let the moon's periods dominate our time keeping. We usually try to combine things which *seem* to be alike, and when they turn out not to mesh, we must scrunch or stretch some of them, or all of them, to make them combine. The question then arises, have we fundamentally altered the pure natural things which we have scrunched and stretched — into something else? Or are they really the same, and we have just taken a bit of the edge off?

The idea of compromise or temperament in music has been hard to accept because of the special place music has held in Western culture for so many centuries. For some reason, philosophically, people believed that music was not a human invention, not an art, but something which existed already in pure form as part of the structure of the universe. Three forms of music (or aspects, we might say) were taught in Medieval universities: *musica humana, musica mundana,* and *musica instrumentalis.* Only the third kind — having to do with instruments made by man — could even be heard by human ears. The other two existed as a result of the perfect reciprocal motions of the fixed stars and the planets, as they spun in their daily dance according to God's perfect laws. Music was part of a beautiful orderly scheme of the natural world, and any of it that was permitted to break through into our dimension must be received with great care. We could observe the laws of number which governed music — but *alter* them?

Songs, in Western music at least, are based upon intervals — the tone distance or sound space between any two notes. Very few songs use only one note. And though the democracy of statistics would show that you *can* sing any number of note combinations, one after another, to make a melody, music has not proven itself to be very democratic: instead there are certain intervals which seem to be more *noticeable* than others. They seem to be ones which more people can put a name to, can remember, and thus can easily repeat. These intervals, the fourth, the fifth and the octave, became bellweathers in music from the very earliest times. Songs tended to coalesce around them. Even when they weren't striving consciously to hit these intervals in their melodies, people couldn't help falling into their sphere of influence. Thus fifths, fourths and octaves became directors and shapers in the musical scale systems which different western cultural groups were formulating. There was a reason for this. These octaves, fifths, fourths (and later, major thirds) — these combinations of musical tones into intervals — have, in addition to the approving judgment of the listening ear, a mathematical "approval rating." Because human beings rely upon numbers to help them define reality, the musical intervals which exhibit simple numerical relationships have come to be called "pure consonant" intervals. In keyboard tuning systems these mathematically-sanctioned, pure consonant intervals are much more important than they are in other aspects of music. Because all temperaments use these intervals as a standard, and then deviate from all or some of them, we need to understand how they work, both numerically and musically, in the formation of our diatonic scale — the scale which we are accustomed to hearing on the piano.

A description of how laws of number work in music, particularly how they define consonant intervals, was made by the Greek mathematician Pythagoras (living approximately 572 to 497 B.C.). He made actual experiments with a single-stringed instrument called a monochord. It is not known exactly what Pythagoras did,* but the result of his work established a hierarchical relationship between small whole numbers and musical intervals. This, in turn, tended to reinforce the idea that purity of consonance is desirable — even necessary — in music.

*sotto voce: Harry Partch, in Genesis of A Music, calls Pythagoras 'that musical Saint Paul of the early Greek world,' who is 'famous for many institutions, all of them legendary or very nearly legendary.' In other words, Pythagoras, and the Greeks in general I should add, are handy 'scapegoats' for us to pin origins upon, but a certain percentage of it is definitely legendary.

Pythagoras discovered that the most perfect musical interval, the one we call the octave, occurs because two tones are vibrating in a 2 to 1 relationship (the higher tone moving twice as fast as the lower tone). The interval of the fifth was nicely taken care of with the next superparticular ratio, the one comprised of a 2 and a 3 (the top tone vibrates 3 times every time the bottom tone vibrates twice), and the interval of the fourth manifests itself similarly with frequencies which factor into 3 and 4. These were, apparently, the most common "pure" intervals used in the music of Pythagoras' time. He could have gone one number and one superparticular ratio further — 5 to 4 — and described the pure major third, but he did not. Perhaps that is just as well, since it can be said that the use of thirds in Western music — particularly on keyboards — in a sense brought about an "overload" in the system, and created the necessity for temperaments. But that was 1000 years or so after Pythagoras.

This experiment with a monochord seemed to confirm nicely the notion that nature works in beautiful, simple, small whole numbers. These numbers sing pure sounds in combination. Any combinations in between (say, 1.73:2 instead of 1:2) is less pure and not worth the same kind of attention. Whatever the Greek people may have been playing on their four-stringed kitharas and other instruments before Pythagoras, after his discoveries their music was described more formally by a scale system based upon octaves, fifths and fourths. Musicians at least had a standard to follow in tuning their instruments, and music theorists could with some satisfaction remind themselves that there was heaven-sent order underlying the chaos that music sometimes seemed to provide.

Before we return to the piano and how it is tuned, let us digress a bit more about small whole numbers. Their seemingly quixotic behavior in music is an endless source of fascination.

Tuner's Monologue

"I hereby declare this piano to be tuned!" — *If tuning a piano is not an exact science (it is neither exact, nor a science, exactly) then how does the tuner know when the piano is "done"?*

She could, after all, keep going indefinitely. The ear is a very discriminating instrument. It can always find fault. There is a waver in that octave, a twang in that unison. Fix this interval, go over those chords again, and again. Will I be here forever? (Lunchtime recedes into the distance, irretrievable.)

It all goes back to the beginning. If the beginning was right, then, eventually, there will be an ending. A tuned piano can be declared.

Divertimento on Numbers

"Sense is an uncertain guide. Numbers cannot fail."
Pythagoras

"Musical patterns elevate certain numbers to a prominence pure number theory would not accord them."
McClain, *The Myth of Invariance*

Mythology and the stories, songs and dances which express it, are full of small whole numbers. Each number from one to five has a whole host of ideas and symbols attached to it. *One* represents wholeness, God, the beginning, the male (or sometimes female) principle, uniqueness. *Two* represents good and evil, all opposites, twin gods, yin and yang, the (sometimes) female principle, in it is contained the concept of symmetry which underlies physics, and with it comes a simple notion of harmony in duplication. Without two we would not know one from the other. With *Three* the picture grows more complex: there is now the possibility of discord, of asymmetry; the idea of many begins to unfold; yet at the same time, three is more stable than two as a structural delineator (triangles, a grand piano has three legs), and without the three spatial dimensions life on Earth could not exist. *Four*, although a duplication of two, is not thought of that way. Many religions attach especial importance to the four directions, the four winds, the four seasons; four is used often as a basis for

clan divisions in tribal cultures; medieval theology iter-
ated the four apostles of the gospel, the four horsemen
of the apocalypse.

Numbers one, two, three and four are "numbers of
the spheres;" they carry on their symbolic duties in a
highly abstract realm. Number five, like Prometheus,
touches Earth while retaining divine status. In addition
to being the symbol (not surprisingly) for specific five-
fold patterns in nature (the hand, certain flowers), five
came to stand for the "human" as opposed to the "divine" in philosophy. Later, in the Middle Ages (and perhaps in some odd way five is responsible), number five
was associated with all that is earthly, organic, physical
− especially human love and procreation.

Mythology, philosophy, religion and folklore delight
in the constant interplay of these first few numbers.
When they are realized in symbolic ways, it is difficult,
if not impossible, to separate the number from what it
stands for. The number is not functioning simply as a
counting device, to make things follow one another in
sequence. Rather the number is grasped all at once with
the idea. You would think of Five as different from
Four or Three in the same way that your sister is different from your aunt.

Not so with the higher numbers. After nine (in fact,
the process begins sooner than nine. If someone flashes
a card before you with four dots on it, for a fraction of
a second, you would probably recognize four, even
though you didn't have time to count. But if they flash
a card with seven or eight, you might not.) After nine,
or slightly before, most people can no longer comprehend a number as a whole, but must stop and break it

down into groups, or count up one by one. The few becomes the many. Instead of naming we make the transition over to counting. This requires a different part of the mind, a different attitude, and is done for a different purpose. We do not cherish seven million four hundred and forty thousand one hundred twenty eight in the same way we do a seven.

Music, too, cherishes small whole numbers. Its beauty lies, partly at least, in the clumps of twos and threes which are at the heart of its structure. But music takes the ones and twos and threes and fours and fives and combines them into ratios: 1:2, 2:3, 3:4, 4:5, and 5:6. These ratios then function in themselves as new wholes.

Here is a chart of the pure consonant intervals which figure prominently in our diatonic scale. They are mathematically "pure" because they are fashioned out of small whole number ratios. They are acoustically "pure" because when struck, the individual tones make patterns which do not interfere with one another, but cancel and reinforce one another so that a listener hears no extraneous throbbing sounds or "beats." Only consonant intervals are beatless.

Relationships of Consonant Intervals

Interval	Example (C-major scale)	Ratio (Relationship of frequencies between the fundamental and the note)
Octave	C - C'	1:2
Fifth	C - G	2:3
Fourth	C - F	3:4
Major Third	C - E	4:5
Minor Third	C - E-flat	5:6
Major Sixth	C - A	3:5
Minor Sixth	C - A-flat	5:8

In music, numbers exhibit a behavior that is peculiar to music. They seek to remain stable, aloof, as serene inhabitants of their mathematical realm. But they are constantly tugged upon by the melodies in which they are enmeshed. Their musical context lends them an identity, both alone and in rational combinations, which identity does not truly exist for them elsewhere.

To understand how these ratios work in music, it is necessary to be able to shift slightly the usual way in which you are taught to think of them. One-half, one-third, two-thirds, etc. we usually understand to denote amount, or part-of-the-whole. It is an encroachment into the pie.

But it can also mean a relationship between two distinct, individually-vibrating tones in music. As such, the numbers are a unit, denoting the tension-of-the-proportion in the musical interval. As such, *the interval came first*, and the numerical ratio simply happens to fit its pattern. It is important to remember this point.

As a unit ratio in music, the numbers represent a balance. A musical interval, when expressed as a ratio of two individually-vibrating notes, is not the same as a fraction. The interval of the fifth is not two-thirds of some whole, which we would call one; the fifth is a whole in itself. The two notes which comprise the fifth are "two-to-threeing" together.

Each consonant interval can be thought of as part of a system — a system which is self-contained and entire. It probably makes a geometric shape, somewhere in a universal conceptual space. But we insist upon pulling in these interval-shapes and making them do something artistic rather than natural; we combine them in a straight line on our keyboards, and not only that, we limit their natural boundaries by stuffing them into a kind of acoustical container — the octave.

C	C#	D	D#	E	F	F#	G	G#	A	A#	B	C
8	8.46	8.96	9.49	10.06	10.66	11.30	11.97	12.68	13.44	14.24	15.10	16

→ halfway

A Space-Time Diagram

Translating time (vibration frequency) into space (width of keys on a piano keyboard tuned in equal temperament)

How the piano keyboard would look if each key width in one octave reflected accurately the frequency increase of its note. Each note vibrates at a frequency which is the frequency of the note below it, multiplied by the twelfth root of 2, or approximately 1.0594631.

Fifth Interval

"At this time there was no scale in our meaning of an exact series of fixed pitches. There was instead a mode, or melodic series of unequal intervals, including tones of mutable pitch; the performer adjusted these mutable tones by microtonal deviations to satisfy the harmonic requirements of the melody."

> (Peter Yates, describing Western music prior to the 16th century, in *Twentieth Century Music*)

"If a bushel of corn turned out upon the floor makes a noise, each grain and each part of each grain must make a noise likewise, but, in fact, it is not so."

> (one of Zeno's paradoxes)

For blackbirds sitting on a telephone line, there is a natural territorial distance which they insist shall intervene from one bird to the next. The birds make a scale,

45

there on the wire, with biologically mandated intervals. We do not use all possible musical "blackbirds" which could be stuffed, one after another, onto our octave "wire." We hear best and most happily (in the West, at least) when our adjacent notes have an established territory. Each note must be a whole in itself, it cannot trail bits and pieces of the one behind. Our music does not slide (not yet, not yet). It makes quantum jumps. The space between notes remains silent.

But what is that space? Our ears can comfortably distinguish about 40 or 50 "differences" in musical tone between a fundamental and its octave, but we have chosen to make our music with only 12 notes (13, if you count the octave note over again).*

It would seem to be a happy coincidence that the 'pure consonant intervals which kept occurring naturally

---

*sotto voce: Many other scale systems have been suggested during the history of western music, and many instruments built using them. A popular number is 19, which would allow sharps and flats to co-exist on the same keyboard. Some theorists insist 43 is the ideal number of keys to allow "correct tuning" in all intervals, others have suggested 53. Devising a scale system is done rather the same way language is invented: namely, the grammar comes along later, after people are already speaking. Thus, the scale is recognized and described after people have been playing music for quite a while. After that, the language, or the music, can be altered, if there are powerful enough theoreticians, scholars, churchmen, politicians who decide to impose their grammar, or their scale, upon the culture.

in songs and on instruments, also happened to be the easiest to express mathematically. However, the smallest and most-often-used intervals (in melodies, at least), which are the whole tones and half tones, turned out *not* to be mathematically very manageable. From a piano tuner's point of view, a semitone and a whole tone are not "pure" — that is, the beats cannot be tuned out of either of these intervals. Therefore, they cannot be used to determine the character of the temperament. Nor were they used to determine the diatonic scale itself.

If you look again at a piano keyboard and start up the scale from C, the next note is C-sharp or D-flat. On the piano it is an "enharmonic," which means its tone is a compromise between a true C-sharp and true D-flat, so that it can be used for either. This is something that equal temperament has done. However, supposing that the black note above C really were a C-sharp (as it is in some of the alternate temperaments). What makes it a C-sharp? It does not gain its identity because somebody hums a C, and then hums the next tone "higher." No, the identity of this C-sharp comes because it is a perfect fifth with either the F-sharp below, or the G-sharp above; or because it forms a major third with the A below, or the E above. The notes in our scale ascend and descend in tones and semitones, but each note in the scale, in a sense, "flew in from somewhere else"; that is, the notes didn't come into existence one after another as they appear to our eyes, but rather because each of them is "three-to-twoing" or "five-to-fouring" or "four-to-threeing" with its consonant partner.

Pythagoras, poor chap, probably expected that there would be a "right" number of notes which would fit inevitably between the fundamental and its octave. He built a scale using the fifth and fourth as the governing intervals by which individual notes were generated. The result was the eight-tone, diatonic scale with its peculiar tone-tone-semitone, tone-tone-tone-semitone pattern — a kind of lopsided pattern to fit inside the symmetrical, 2 to 1 octave.

However, Pythagoras paid little attention to the pure consonant interval generated by number 5 — the major third. He simply couldn't find place for pure thirds in his tuning system. Thus, when thirds did occur in music using the Pythagorean scales, they made beats, which meant they were distorted away from their pure form. For many hundreds of years the third was thought of as ugly, or slightly profane, and so its lack of purity in the tuning system did not bother anyone very much.

But why should this be? Why the conflict?

Much as people would like to think of music as something sacred, handed down ready made from On High — it is not. Music is an invention of man; it is not *there* (somewhere) already. Therefore, although right from the start people kept discovering the consonant intervals — unisons, octaves, fifths, fourths, and later thirds and sixths — and bringing them up like glistening shells from the beach to set with reverence among their musical offerings, right from the start these intervals did not get along with one another. In combination they quarreled; they made beats, or worse than that, they made ugly howls and were called "wolves." Either there was more to music than just numbers, or the numbers themselves were making trouble. Actually, it was both.

Tuner's Monologue

In the beginning — Like a fish, a piano forgets easily. It does not matter whether this piano and I have met before. I address it, even before I open the lid. The listening begins with my eyes, then my hands. I am hushed before it, waiting . . . . . .

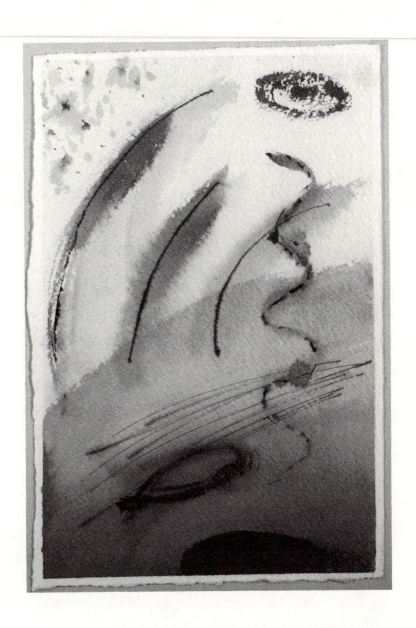

Sixth Interval

"When that the general is not like the hive
To whom the foragers shall all repair,
What honey is expected? Degree being vizarded,
The unworthiest shows as fairly in the mask.
The heavens themselves, the planets and this center,
Observe degree, priority, and place,
Insisture, course, proportion, season, form,
Office and custom, in all line of order . . . .
    But when the planets
In evil mixture to disorder wander,
What plagues and what portents, what mutiny,
What raging of the sea, shaking of earth,
Commotion in the winds, frights, changes, horrors,
Divert and crack, rend and deracinate,
The unity and married calm of states
Quite from their fixure! Oh, when degree is shaked,
Which is the ladder to all high designs,
The enterprise is sick! . . . .
Take but degree away, untune that string,
And hark, what discord follows!"

(Shakespeare — Troilus and Cressida
Act I, Scene 3)

If music can be said to be a language based upon numbers, then the quixotic behavior of numbers-in-combination becomes mirrored in musical scales. The reason we need to temper our scales is one having to do with numbers, but it is not easy to identify a single culprit who causes the quarrel between the intervals. Sometimes the problem is defined by pointing out that if you start with a low C on the piano and go up by pure fifths, then by the time you arrive at the top "C," it is actually higher than the bottom C by a small amount, which we call a "comma." (This means the circle of fifths is actually a spiral.) Thus, in order to stuff all the notes obtained by all these fifths into a single octave, we must scrunch, or temper, the fifths.

Or, the whole thing could be blamed on the thirds.

This seems to make more sense to me, since number 5, which is responsible for bringing us the third, comes along somewhat like the trickster in folklore — a number which has tumbled out of the sky and prefers to dance to earthly rhythms. The third major is a perfectly bona fide, pure consonant ("just") interval, with a super-particular ratio of 5:4, as you will recall. That means it can exist on a keyboard in pure, beatless form. The legendary Pythagoras was content to let the major third be distorted in his tuning systems so that fifths and fourths could all remain pure, but somewhere back in the Renaissance the balance of musical demands began to shift in favor of the thirds, which were needed in major triads; thus musicians began to demand tuning systems which rendered the third in its pure 5:4 form.

However, on keyboard instruments, this turned out to be too much purity.

Notes on pianos are fixed (from the musician's point of view, if not from the piano tuner's). Therefore, in a major triad (example: C-E-G), each of the three notes *can* be tuned to a frequency which will make the whole triad "pure": that is, the ratio of frequencies of the fifth (G-C) is 3:2, and the ratio of frequencies of the major third (E-C) is 5:4. However, each of these notes also has other duties in other chords. Each must serve as root, third, and fifth in a different triad; and the octaves of each note must remain pure, up and down the keyboard. Somewhere on the way from Pythagoras' eight-tone diatonic scale to the twelve tones our tradition finally bestowed upon us, the system became overloaded; notes began to balk. A single note cannot handle too many relationships; it is like trying to be an uncle and a nephew to the same person.

In the diatonic music system to which we are accustomed, with its vertical harmonies, the major third is essential. And yet because five comes after one, two, three, and four, the third must always defer to the octave, fifth and fourth in this system. This means that the third bears the onus of responsibility for bringing so poignantly to the ear's attention the problem of how to combine all the consonant intervals in a 12-tone scale. It is the culprit and the scapegoat. As the third goes, so goes the temperament, and from that, to a large degree, so goes the whole character of the music.

So, if all the pure consonant intervals cannot fit into the music we choose to make, how do we decide where and how much to compromise? Must the choices be arbitrary — or can we let nature be the artist?

Searching nature for the perfect tuning system does

not suffice. (A keyboard is not a "natural" phenome-non.) There is not one natural scale, but many: one can be made from the partials of a vibrating string; one can be built from a series of superparticular ratios; one can be created out of a spiral of fifths, or thirds. All of these ways of "finding" a scale seem to have internal consistency. However, only a few of the notes derived by these natural-numbers games are equivalent to one another; the scales are largely mutually exclusive. And, none of these mathematically-derived natural systems seems to allow for a proper grammar to describe the music that is being actually made in the world out there.

That music is governed by still another natural scale, which also can generate as many notes as you wish to give name to. This is the folk scale, the scale of the ear and the heart, the scale of whim and tradition. Here the notes need not be named, need not have fixed identity, the octave need not prevail with its sere imperative. Notes can appear and disappear like subatomic particles in a cloud chamber, never the same way twice. In this scale, all the odd and even intervals can cavort joyfully in a magnificent rhapsody, bringing the loops of their helixes down to our hearing range, and creating thousand-faceted melodies, each one a nonpareil. Inter-vals and notes have areas, here, not distinct place. The blackbirds blur, teeter and wobble on the line — or perhaps not on the line. This "scale" of the ear and heart is always there, exerting its pressure at the melodic end of the musical spectrum. The music made thus is governed by some intuitive laws of probability which may or may not conform to the harmonies of pure number.

Most music reflects some kind of compromise between natural scales. If the notes are fixed, as on keyboard instruments, the intervals cannot all be pure. If all intervals are played purely, the notes cannot be fixed, but must be able to shift slightly up or down at a moment's notice, as on a violin or with a human voice. The more intervals, the more notes needed, and the more tension in the scale.

No instrument humanly possible to design or to play could have all the intervals we wish to play on our piano keyboard tuned according to any "natural" scale. So, when we make the final, specific discriminating decisions about precisely what the identity of each note is going to be, we do so by a set of deliberate distortions — and call the result a temperament.

Tuner's Monologue

The temperament — opening — We must come to an understanding, this piano and I. I like a slow temperament, and always try in the first three intervals to see whether this piano will agree. Often it does not. Especially the newer ones — they tend to go for the fast beats. Sigh. I test all the possibilities, and settle on the one which is in the piano's heart. We will weave our temperament around this, the piano and I, and it will be good nevertheless.

Seventh Interval

"Forty years after the death of Mersenne, in 1688, the first organ was tuned in accordance with his formula for Equal Temperament . . . thus setting the Western stage for nearly three hundred years of music's 'golden age,' the classroom for the complete divorcement of the science of music from music theory, the concert hall for the benevolent fraud of equally-tempered modulation, the radios of x million American homes for a twenty-five-year siege by the industrialized harmony-armies of mediocrity, and else we know not what."

Harry Partch (*Genesis of a Music*)

In practice, then, a temperament is a system of deliberate altering of intervals away from their pure, small-whole-number ratios, in order to increase the overall number of intervals which can be played in tolerable harmony. It takes a piano tuner to make the final specific decisions about the pitch identity of each note on the keyboard. Equal temperament is the pattern which she casts before her as a guide. It is not an arbitrary guide: each note has its proper and correct frequency (with the standard, A above middle C, defined at 440 cycles per second), and the tuner is supposed to come as close as humanly possible to the proper and correct frequencies when she tunes.

Equal temperament is a benign and homogeneous phenomenon to impose upon a piano. Although the pure consonant intervals, except the octave, are indeed all being *distorted* (tempered), the distortions (temperings) are "equal" — that is, all similar intervals have the same amount of "edge" knocked off. A pure fifth, as you will recall, has a frequency ratio of 3:2: all fifths in the equal tempered scale are irrational, but their non-ratio is approximately 2.996:2. This small distortion, which amounts to about a third of one percent, is not enough to make anyone wince.

The tuner with her trained ear works in a very narrow dimension indeed, a place most people do not know exists. She is striving to extend, just a little, the definition of "perfect fifth" and "perfect fourth" and the rest of the pure consonant intervals by making them "for practical purposes" instead of absolutely correct.* She tempers them, in the center of the piano, according to her pattern: the fifths slightly narrow so they make a sound like a gentle sigh; the fourths a bit wide, so they are starting to make a "wow"; and the major thirds wide enough so they make a regular "wuh-wuh-wuh" beating

*see page 63.

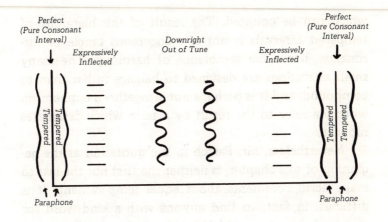

*The Greeks had a specific word "paraphone" to describe a tone which sounds on the way between consonance and dissonance. By this (according to our interpretation) they meant a tone which, when struck as part of an interval, gave the impression of consonance, even though it was not making a pure, rational interval. In other words, a "paraphone" created a tempered interval. The question is, how far can an interval be stretched (tempered) before listeners call it "dissonant" or "out of tune"? Mark Lindley's designation for some of the categories on the chart above are: "perfect," "expressively inflected" and "downright out-of-tune." Equal temperament does not, strictly speaking, use "expressively inflected" intervals, but rather sticks with "paraphones" — that is, intervals which are meant to fool the ear. Even the major and minor thirds, which are far enough from pure to be "expressively inflected," are subsumed into the driving musical imperative behind equal temperament, which is to give an overall impression of weightlessness and transparency.

which can be counted. The result of this hierarchy of tempered intervals is not one enormous tangle of dissonance, but a fair semblance of harmony. The many small alterations are designed to balance rather than to compound, and it is perhaps not altogether a euphemism when we refer to the result by a term which designates rapport.

Nevertheless, Mr. Partch in the quotation at the beginning of this chapter, is neither the first nor the last to make acrid comments about equal temperament. It is difficult, in fact, to find anyone with a kind word for this tuning system, which has been the dominant one for Western music for 150 years, and continues to be, despite predictions that it is on its way out. How, then, did it manage to crowd out its competitors? What do alternative temperaments have to offer that may have been superior?

All temperaments exist within the framework of the diatonic scale — that is, the scale whose harmonies and melodies both are dependent upon the musical tension arising from the relationships between the fifths, fourths and thirds which are the skeleton of the scale. It is not an arbitrary arrangement, as we have seen, but one which has both mathematical and aesthetic justification of long standing.

Thus a temperament is a subtle kind of thing — a sub-species of a single scale. This would seem to mean that the scale defines the rules and the temperament carries them out. A temperament might be just a "polishing" effect, and not worth consideration as a thing with any power of its own. This is how we think of equal temperament — when we think of it at all — as a kind of bland algorithm for Something Higher, but surely with nothing to say for itself. After all, how much influence can one third of one percent exert upon an entire musical system?

However, when we examine the predecessors of equal temperament, we find that they fall into several general categories which are mutually exclusive enough to prompt the question: which comes first, the temperament or the music?

The first tuning systems in Europe on keyboard instruments, the Pythagorean tunings, did not involve deliberate tempering at all. Unlike earlier civilizations, medieval Europeans resisted the negative aspect of tempered tuning, which is the notion that you must "distort" something away from its pure form — even if the distortion amounts to only a sliver of a percent. As long as there were only eight notes to a scale (the ecclesiastical modes), it was possible to move around the octave, tuning as many pure fifths as possible, and pile the leftover disharmonies onto the thirds. The fact that the thirds then turned out to be quite sharp (they had a ratio of 81:64 instead of 5:4), was apparently not thought of as tempering. There is a fine line between recognizing something which happens inevitably, as a result, and something which you do *first*, on purpose.

As the original eight-tone scale grew gradually to twelve, the small leftover disharmonies compounded, until at last they were no longer just a few acceptably-sharp major thirds, but instead became unacceptable, non-musically-useful diminished sixths and augmented seconds which were quite obviously out of place (the wolf intervals). It is assumed that musicians simply tried to avoid playing the wolf intervals, or covered them up with ornamentation.*

A second non-tempered tuning system which existed in theory at least, was called "just intonation." The mandate of just intonation tuning is: tune all consonant intervals possible, including major thirds, pure. Unlike Pythagorean tuning, the just tunings tried to include some pure major thirds in with the pure fourths and fifths. But the same basic problem existed with just intonation as with Pythagorean tuning — where to put the wolves.

Apparently, throughout the Middle Ages and even later, until the piano was invented (perhaps), the ideal of just intonation was maintained, even though it was obvious that there was not enough "justness" for all the music that people wanted to play. A high price was paid for the small shining circle of pure triads in the increasingly wobbly ripples which emanated from its center. But, then, who knows what people were hearing? Before the piano, instruments were quieter, their overtone structures different. Perhaps listeners kidded themselves

---

*sotto voce: Although for each individual temperament, there was usually a single interval which was considered aberrant enough to be called a "wolf," there were others narrow or wide to a degree which made them noticeably "off the mark." Music composed during the time when meantone temperament was in common use seems to indicate that both the wolf intervals and the other, "expressively inflected," intervals, were carefully exploited for musical interest; thus ornamentation was only one way of "handling" dissonance.

in a different way than we do now; perhaps they waited for the pure intervals, which probably occurred frequently, and lumped everything else into the category of outer darkness. Evil is necessary, they may have thought, to make Good shine.

Meantone temperament is the name given to the first system (as far as we know) which deliberately tempered intervals. The intervals which were tempered were the fifths, and this was done chiefly to allow a larger number of major thirds to remain pure (or nearly so), because triads were very important in the evolving major-minor tonality system. Various "meantone" temperaments were devised by enthusiastic entrepreneurs often more addicted to mathematics than to music, but the idea behind it seemed to be that it was permissable to distort fifths in order to bring those awful Pythagorean thirds down from being so sharp. The result apparently allowed for music written in keys with only a couple or three sharps or flats to sound especially familiar and sweet, while at the same time the "bad" intervals around the edges could be called into service for contrast.

Another way of altering fifths led to various "irregular" temperaments. They came into use, generally, later than the meantones – in the 18th century. By this time equal temperament, which had been invented, or discovered, on paper many times over (the Chinese found it first), was in practical use on lutes and viols and other fretted stringed instruments. As ensemble music grew in importance, keyboard instruments tuned in meantone did not blend with the instruments built to equal temperament. The irregular temperaments tried to edge away from the problem by easing the extreme distinction between consonance and dissonance found in meantone temperaments. It was an attempt to have your cake and eat it too — not totally to relinquish the ideal of pure intonation upheld by earlier tunings and temperaments, yet not to give up some variety of dissonance also. The wolves were gone, but there remained enough "prickly" intervals to tweak the ear.

Equal temperament as a tuning system was first described in practical detail so far as we know by the blind music theorist Francisco Salinas in 1577. (He also invented several meantone temperaments about the same time.) What is "equal" in equal temperament is the size of the semitone; each of the twelve tones in the octave is the same tone "distance" from the one on either side. This distance is an irrational number, the twelfth root of 2. By using this quantity to retain geometrical balance, the pure octave ratio 2:1 can be maintained up and down the scale, with 12 notes in between all evenly spaced (like blackbirds). In a sense, then, you can say the equal-tempered scale *is* defined by a non-consonant interval, even though a piano tuner still arrives at her equal semitones by tuning fifths, fourths and thirds. This relentless equality of semitones means that no other interval within the octave is quite pure. It is an impurity to which we have grown accustomed. Hardly anyone but a piano tuner can hear the distortions in the fifths and fourths; in the major and minor thirds they are more obvious. But in a well-tuned piano, the beats in the thirds seem to cancel each other out during the playing of triads, giving an impression of purity. Dissonance is spread very thinly indeed in the democratic, equally tempered scale.

Equal temperament arrived with the piano. If it is looked upon in the way it first appeared, as a compromise, it might not immediately seem to be a deliberate and mathematically exact deviation from purity. It might not seem permissive; might not seem to be irrationality on purpose. But there is no such thing as "a little bit equal." The earlier ideal in tempered and non-tempered tuning systems had always been to retain at least a few pure harmonic intervals. So long as a modicum of perfection was held on to, a whole musical framework could be maintained, However, once pure — mathematically exact and rational — harmony was relinquished as the underlying mandate of a tuning system, then whatever replaced it was not just a phase of the old order, but a new order entirely.

And though equalizing the semitones on a keyboard instrument so that all keys of the major-minor tonality system can be played without apprehension is, in the light of twentieth-century Western music, a limiting rather than an innovative arrangement, it has been something which pushed our music along a certain path for a certain time.*

From the point of view of a musician several hundred years ago, trained in a tradition in which musical scales were tinged with the Divine (Popes even issued statements about what notes could and could not be used in musical compositions), an equal-tempered scale might — if examined closely — represent something akin to heresy. Our scales come trailing clouds of glory from

*sotto voce: Please refer to "A Temperament 'Salad' " on page 97 (Appendix).

the music of the spheres (this musician thought). They are ordained: something to be discovered, not made. Yet the piano tuner is not just temporarily deviating from purity out of musical necessity — rather she is setting a temperament whose perfection *is* its inexactness. Where might such an idea lead?

Tuner's Monologue

The Temperament — middle — *Circling and circling,
I mold my temperament, urging the unruly into balance.
Each interval must blend with the next interval, which
must blend with the next . . . and back to the beginning.
In the center there is a secret, for only this piano and I
know where the leftovers went. There is a well we both
make, to draw them. It is Nowhere.*

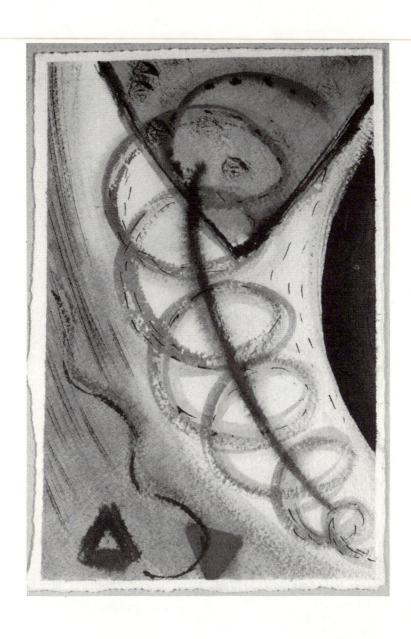

Eighth Interval

"How nature loves the incomplete. She knows
If she drew a conclusion it would finish her.
But, O God, for one round Amen!"

Christopher Fry (*Venus Observed*)

It all depends upon what we mean by exact.

Our equal temperament, which defines and regulates much of our music other than just that on the piano, is an amalgamation of parts. Each of them, if not confined in time and space, might relapse into purity. We want to make music in a certain way, so we patch the parts together and stand far enough away so as not to notice the cracks.

The purist begins to weep. For when a piano is tuned in equal temperament, it sounds fine. The ear *can* detect the tell-tale beats, but chooses not to. How can that be? What have we done? In inventing the piano, have we exposed ourselves as a planet of impostors who derive

our acoustical pleasures from an abominable approxima-
tion? Do we *prefer* almost, to exact, harmony?

I spoke in the Seventh Interval of temperaments as a
sub-species of a scale. This would seem to keep them for
sure in a reactionary role to the whims of music. However, if you spread out all the keyboard tuning systems
end to end, and examine them in terms of their "purity"
or "exactness" level, something interesting shows up.

Just intonation, at one end of this new spectrum,
contains a maximum of "pure" or rational intervals.
Total purity is its standard, and while this is not possible
on keyboard instruments, as we have seen, it is possible
in singing and on unfretted stringed instruments. Therefore, it is a system which can be realized in some music.
Equal temperament, at the other end of the spectrum,
has almost *none* of its intervals "pure" or rational (the
octave being the exception). Yet the two systems, opposite though they be, have in common a way of almost
neutralizing the music that is played under their influence. Depending on your taste, you might call the result
monotonous — or ethereal.

We seem to be making a new distinction here. We
had always assumed that our familiar diatonic scale, and
the major-minor tonality system which accompanies it,
existed apart from, not because of, the rather arcane
matter of how the harpsichord (or piano) was tuned. Yet
the very idea of being able to speak truly of the "key"
in which something is composed, and have the term retain meaning, assumes there is a distinction between
sharps and flats in a scale. In the meantone temperaments such a distinction was present, although there is
no way that a single meantone temperament, limited by

a 12-tone octave, could include more than a fraction of the 24 "keys" the system theoretically allows for.

Nevertheless, although it is not strictly clear to me exactly how the "key of B-flat", (for example) was immediately recognizable as itself and nothing else, it is certain that much livelier distinctions existed from one key to another back when the meantone and irregular temperaments were in common use. After equal temperament came along and imposed the enharmonic compromise upon the accidentals, then the notion of what "key" a piece was composed in became essentially meaningless. For, just as a temperament is a sub-species of a scale,* so a "key" is a sort of sub-species of a mode (the diatonic mode). Without the variety of intervals to identify the "key," the term lapses into no more than an arbitrary theoretical "handle" for a composer to use in identifying his piece, and we must grope for variety in other ways. Ironically, then, by increasing the *number* of chords we can play harmoniously, we have decreased the *kinds* of chords we can play. Is there now only one Great Melody that all composers take snippings from?

Let us look just a bit more closely at equal temperament's predecessors, and what weakness they must have displayed to be displaced by something so bland, so irrational, so inexact.

One reason keyboard instruments are important is that the distinction between consonance and dissonance is immediately and urgently present on them, since they permit a single performer to realize vertical harmony

*sotto voce: If you need a reminder about this, please see page 64 above.

(that is, chords). Prior to equal temperament, a composer could exploit various degrees of dissonance in his/her composition — even though there was an implicit artistic decree which limited the quantity — if not the actual balance — of this dissonance. And prior to the piano, a temperament could be modulated with relative ease in order to accommodate the balance of harmonies desired by the composer.

There remains, of course, a huge difference, no matter what, between the subtle and quick switches in intonation possible in instruments like violins and human voices, and the no-less-subtle but much less quick switches in intonation possible on a harpsichord. Therefore, if a composer several hundred years ago chose to modulate within a single composition (substituting, for example, an A-flat for what would usually be a G-sharp), he would have to take his lumps, so to speak, in the fact that the keyboard would not make the switch. Thus, a great deal of keyboard music, even in times of more diverse temperaments, was still modulated "on paper only"; composers then, as now, were to some degree composing for instruments not yet invented.* Never-

*sotto voce: Some of these instruments were, indeed, invented. Beginning with the medieval organs built with split keys to eliminate "wolf" intervals in standard meantone temperament, many organs were built which split various keys to accommodate both true sharps and true flats. Numerous experimental keyboards have been invented for harpsichords, pianos and other instruments, including the famous "push-button" keyboard of Paul von Janko in 1882. Harry Partch is a contemporary composer who invented a keyboard to play his own compositions.

theless in earlier times the tuner was not a separate person who came in before the performance: the tuner and composer (performer) were one and the same individual. I imagine the music of these times was influenced by the knowledge that a performer had the ability to change Mr. Hyde (a wolf interval) into Dr. Jekyll by just a flick of the wrist.

It is theoretically possible, also, to "modulate" an entire temperament in one fell swoop: that is, to shift the pattern of consonances and dissonances from the acoustic tonality of C major in which temperaments are normally tuned, to any other "key." But this, too, would change the color of the "key" system into black and white — or into invisibility.

The desire to modulate, and the desire to expand the key signatures from a few flats and sharps into four or more, was a driving force in music, apparently, from the sixteenth century to the nineteenth. And it is this drive for diversity which we hold responsible for the rise of equal temperament. Yet, why would musicians opt for a temperament which, rather than taking them to an infinity of "key" possibilities, instead was taking them to *one* possibility? Their ears told them what was happening; they complained; they resisted; it happened perforce.

Part of the reason, I think, may have been a characteristic of the piano. On this new instrument it was no longer so easy to re-tune an interval on a moment's notice to modulate the temperament and keep the balance of dissonances closer to the way the composer and performer wanted them. Not so much because a single piano tuning pin is significantly harder to move than a harpsichord pin, but because the piano as a whole is more difficult to tune – at least it became so by the end of the 18th century. Thus there may have developed a universal sense among musicians that their little temper-. ament modulations – which amounted to key changes – were no longer possible. This kind of awe before new technology is certainly prevalent in our own time, and keeps many of us from accomplishing simple repair tasks that actually require a minimum of knowledge and skill. The piano may have, as it evolved into a monster with iron in its heart, inspired this kind of technology-grip among composers and performers. And if the little tuning modulations stopped, then the music probably started exhibiting more sour chords and "bad" transitions. And this, in turn, would have caused people to demand blander intervals rather than bolder tuners. It is the usual case of taking the easy way out.

Perhaps, then, it was not so much an abhorrence of "wolf" intervals in themselves that caused meantone temperament to be replaced by irregular temperaments, and the final victory of the most regular-irregular temperament of them all – rather it was that the wolves could not be moved around quickly enough any more. A wolf strategically placed is very, very good; a wolf out of place is horrid.

It could be that equal temperament came about by default, just as the whole idea of tempering happened in the first place. For whatever reasons, when we made this temperament our common tuning system some 150 years ago, we discarded wolves and pure intervals all at once. Consonant relationships between notes was not the crucial factor any more; instead, each individual note, like a blackbird, need only stay a certain distance away from its neighbor. This made for a new Ideal. If exact consonance was no longer sought, then what, exactly, was a piano supposed to do?

It is the business of science to get at the nature of things by taking them apart. If they won't come apart by sawing, melting, bombarding, etc., we think them apart. A whole can be understood by examining its parts. And if those parts do not yield the key to the puzzle, well, then, we take *them* apart; for everything can be considered a whole, and each smaller part becomes, in turn, a new whole. If we have the parts all laid out before us, their properties will then be simple to discern. All that remains to understand the whole is to combine the parts, with their measured and defined properties. The exactness of the small will transfer to the larger, and we will know what we're talking about.*

Consider the parts of an equally-tempered scale. Each note, as the scale ascends, vibrates faster than the note below it. How much faster it vibrates is a multiple of the vibrations of the previous note. Rather like compound interest in banking, where a certain fixed per-

---

*sotto voce: Renaissance architect Lenoe Battista Alberti perhaps typifies this attitude in a statement from Book IX of his Ten Books on Architecture (1485): ". . . a compleat Knowledge of a Whole is to be gained by examining the several Parts distinct." This is not the same attitude as "the whole is greater than the sum of its parts." Temperaments, in general, are most definitely greater than the sum of their parts!

centage of interest is given, and each time that percentage is brought to bear, it is multiplying not the original principal, but a multiple of that principal. In order that twelve notes will each sound the exact same amount higher than one another, going up the octave, and that the top note will be vibrating at exactly twice the rate of the fundamental, the notes must have the same "interest" rate. For our tempered scale, that amount is the twelfth root of two, and cannot be expressed as a simple whole number, or as a ratio. Therefore, in a sense it is inexact, and in the same sense the intervals between notes are doomed to be forever parts, never wholes, never finished, but trailing their remainders on out and out into infinity in one of those awful curves which keeps approaching a line, but never reaching it.

The equal-tempered scale is another in a long line of attempts to be specific in defining and confining what we call music. Something along the way keeps eluding us. We can never seem to zero in on a whole which includes all the parts we want. It may be that music cannot be fully and satisfactorily understood this way. One of the reasons understanding does not come automatically with dissection and measurement may be a physical one. At a certain level some things are always parts, never wholes; others are always wholes, never parts. Some sub-atomic "particles" in physics seem to be unstructured. There is a sense in which every particle is always the *same* one over and over again—a perpetual, indivisible whole. By the same token, the quark in physics may embody the idea of absolute partness. A quark may not exist except in its part phase; it is perhaps not a thing in itself, subject to isolation, but only *aspect* in the raw.

Those things which can be taken apart and measured are explained in terms of a scale. That which for some reason cannot be compared to something else, and its identity thus extracted, is said to be non-scalar. Every physical dimension seems to have its non-scalar entities, which science and philosophy use as invariant beacons by which to guide them through darkness. The speed of light is non-scalar.

Perhaps the piano keyboard is trying to tell us something. Although its outward appearance is serene and level, it is seething with possibilities. Because the whole realm of tempered intervals is a very narrow one, and our subject might seem in a way to be an argument about angels on the head of a pin, nevertheless it is in the microcosm that clues must be found to explain events of larger magnitude. Genes are very small (if they can even be said to be "things" at all), yet they determine the nature of each individual human being; the question of the origin of the universe, at some times at least, has hinged upon a determination of the mass of a supposedly massless particle — the neutrino. In that tiny, almost indiscernible area where a pure consonant interval swells and throbs its way into being a tempered interval, could there lie perhaps another clue? It may be that the svelte and intoxicating purity which tradition has told us is the underpinning of what most of us recognize as music — perhaps does not truly exist in the way we have always cherished.

Tuner's Monologue

The Temperament — closing — Now we are coming around the circle of fifths. Closing my eyes, I play my favorite temperament chords: A minor, F-sharp major, A-flat minor, A major. As they sound, the chords should fall through the floor. It is as though I and this piano are in an immense hall, and the sounds begin high in the ceiling . . . float down through us, and out again, beneath. We do not begin them; they were there already. That is how you know the temperament is ready.

Ninth Interval

". . . O, but everyone
Was a bird; and the song was wordless; the
singing will never be done."

(Siegfried Sassoon, "Everyone Sang")

A perfectly-tuned concert grand sings magnificently. For the listener, the music seems to arrive, all at once, as though it came from nowhere, and suddenly arose inside like a new spring. The listener may weep with the music, he may laugh, his body and heart may swell with an almost painful exultation. But where is the piano? The tuner has done well; she has made the piano sound so good that nobody notices it any more. Dragon, piano, tuner, ears — all have vanished together, and only the music remains.

This was not supposed to happen — if we continue to operate on a principle that perfect means exact, and exact is better than almost.

We are well aware of the inexactness of equal temperament. But putting aside the temperament for a
moment, there are other impediments to the joy of
listening to piano music. No sound comes to our ears
without distortion. The speakers on our stereo systems
distort, the walls of the room distort, our ears distort,
and the very fact of encapsulating a fragment of music
in a recording, some would say, is a kind of distortion.
Inside the piano there are a thousand irregularities: 'tis
the nature of the beast.

Despite it all, we continue to think we are hearing
something beautiful, and so we are. Our ears, our hearts,
forgive. Music could even be defined by what we happen
to be forgiving at a particular time in history.

Western music has always been closely linked with
numbers in almost all of its aspects — rhythm, melody,
and through the partials, even the quality of the tone.
Thus we support an assumption that numbers define our
music. Yet as any theoretical mathematician can tell
you, numbers themselves are quite unruly, not wholly
understood, and seem capable of combining in quite
arbitrary and promiscuous fashion. The full meaning of
all their combinations is yet to be grasped. Prime numbers remain apparently without pattern, and thus un-
predictable. Which number patterns do we assume music
to be conforming to?

Proportion is a kind of metaphor; it is a way of
identifying the shape of a thing. The sheer rationality of
the superparticular ratios of just musical intervals bonds
the individual frequencies of the top and bottom notes
and gives the interval its tone-shape. Yet our ears can
hear "unjust" intervals and still identify them as intervals

— whether they are unjust due to being tempered or downright out-of-tune. And the judgment of our ears may not always come down in favor of exact purity. We have tolerated "paraphones" in our music for over a century in equal temperament: can we truly say our ears are still being fooled — or have we shifted our percep-·tion, and the range of our preference, to new figure and new ground?

We look at the equally tempered scale on the piano and bog ourselves down with worry about parts and wholes, about why the circle of fifths turns out to be a spiral, about the fractal nature of the space between pure consonance and noticeable dissonance. But we are always counting. Perhaps musical intervals are non-scalar. A temperament is a "Doing" always, never a "Being." And perhaps music, in its full and ultimate inclination, is Being, and thus cannot truly be arrested and defined with the number-jacket of equal tempera-ment, or any other tuning system. These are *aspects* of music, only.

We have inside our heads something we want to do, and we try to do it with metal and wood and strings, and seconds and lengths and widths and tensions, and woofers and tweeters and electronic impulses — all of which is supposed to produce music. With all this en-cumbrance, how can we tell if there is a Music Fairy who visits during the night to turn our hodge-podge into something real — or are we left every morning still putting parts together? What is the acoustical equivalent of light-speed? Is that what we seek to comprehend?

Equal temperament is a view of a nexus where many of the natural aspects of music come together. It is a crossroads, and as such perhaps just as "pure" and "exact" and "natural" as anything else that is imposed upon music, including exact small-whole-number ratios. If music is larger and more pure than all this, then surely there are other aspects not yet received or explored. We did invent music, yes — or did we?

The equally tempered scale which is now used on our pianos may be the eye of calm in a potential hurricane. Music is propelled by a frenzy, which is now contained. Like a slime mold (pardon the comparison), music must renew itself periodically in order to survive. All its parts combine. It shifts place. Its center goes somewhere else. Its Idea gleams in new dress. For a long time people do not even know there has been a change. They keep doing the same thing, not realizing a judge has re-interpreted the law.

Equal temperament and the piano seem to go together. But our music was not born into the world in the shape of a piano — it only seems to be that way. The equally tempered scale which is now used on pianos has held its place for over 150 years, I think, through a marvelous balance between what is and what seems in music. It has kept harmony and frenzy from galloping off in all directions at once, and tearing music asunder. Because of all the things it *is not*, the equally tempered scale is a kind of "secret place" for everyone who listens, and like the Seventh Dragon, achieves in its invisibility, an identity within the imagination of everyone who tries to comprehend it.

We have been at peace in the eye of a hurricane. What will be the great wind of the future? Perhaps we will listen our way, for a time, into a silence beyond song. Perhaps we will evolve, in our instruments and in our souls, until we can truly comprehend an infinite harmonic scale not tempered, which would play music on some instrument we could hear in our listening dreams.

Postlude

This brings us full circle, back to the listening piano tuner leaning over the piano. If setting a temperament were merely a routine skill, it could be done by a deaf robot programmed to count beats. But this book was supposed to tell you what temperament was really about. And I can't consider that task complete until I tell you about unisons.

I think I explained pure consonant intervals, and how a tuner tunes them "pure" by playing them over and over and taking the beats out, before she then makes them a little bit impure again by bringing beats (or mere wavers) back in again. The same thing happens with unisons, except that they are not tempered. In a unison you come as close as is physically and philosophically possible to resolving a paradox: how can two things ever be called "the same"? I think Albert Einstein puzzled over this matter some 80 years ago with motion. He wondered if there were such a thing as a message being received "at the same time" that it was sent. Maybe that is not what Einstein really wondered. But we do use the word "same" in a sloppy way sometimes, to refer to two different events or items, and what we really mean is "equivalent" or "equal."

So, back to unisons. After the piano tuner finishes setting her temperament, she then must make sure that each individual note is tuned in unison. Most notes on the piano use two or three strings to make their sound. And these two or three strings must make the "same" sound (not equal, but the *same*!) It might seem a simple enough matter — after all, you keep making fine adjustments with the tuning hammer until you stop hearing beats. And that is true, as far as it goes. But with unisons it is the same (the same) as with the temperament-as-a-whole: the whole is greater than the sum of its parts. Or, to put it another way, you are not simply getting rid of something bad (beats), you are doing something positive as well. So, unison is not just a place where beats do not exist. What *is* it, then?

I think some other tuners might disagree with me here, so I hasten to say that this is merely my own perception of a unison.

As you tune your unison, and you hear the beats gradually slowing down, there comes a place where they are too slow to count any more. There, they turn into a kind of swelling effect. The beats have stopped, but you have not yet found unison. By now you are far past the point of "tempering" (even though tempering usually involves only a waver, instead of a full-fledged beat). You have entered a dimension in which "pure" and "exact" are measured in some way other than by counting. Intuition takes over here. You are not even using your ears any more in the usual way; they can only take you to the place where the beats stop, and the waver slows down, and the only thing left is a kind of thronging. You are *listening* in a different way than ever before. You have stopped counting. You have stopped hearing with just your ears. You have stopped.

And then, I think, you fall the rest of the way in, to unison. Because there is not a gradual lessening any more, from the waver, which then blends and begins to straighten out, and gradually fades into stillness. No, I think there is an area where you cross — suddenly — and there you *are*. You can never know what happened on the way over, because you were falling. (Is that the way quanta of light come to us through space?)

I think the listening piano tuner has to learn how to fall that last bit; otherwise she will only be getting rid of beats and wavers, but she will not be *doing* anything good at all. And I think the piano's song is right *there*, in the falling-in place, which is the final tempering.

Appendix A

A Temperament "Salad"

In choosing a temperament, the decision-making process is much like one you might use in gourmet cooking. For example, you wish to decide upon a salad dressing. Your first choice, of course, if whether to use dressing or not.* Then, you make the basic selection among different types of dressings: thousand island, oil and vinegar, blue cheese, etc.* If you choose oil and vinegar, then you must decide which kind of oil and which kind of vinegar. But the choices need not stop here.* Your olive oil may be Spanish or Italian; it may come from a particular area of Italy, and be heavy and fruity, or light and mild. Your vinegar may be red or white, and may be flavored with tarragon. Its essence is derived from the grapes from which it is made — like wine. The subtle distinctions call forth the utmost discriminating faculties of your palate. Your well-being is influenced in ways you are not even aware of!

And then, of course, someone forgot to take out the bay leaf. Maybe that is the wolf interval?

*   If you choose a plain salad, you have chosen equal temperament.

*   You must choose between basic types of temperament: meantone, irregular, Pythagorean, just.

*   If you have chosen irregular, now you have to make further distinctions: Werkmeister, French ordinaire, Bendeler . . . . . . etc.

Appendix B

Table of just ("pure") intervals, and the same intervals in tempered form in a variety of scales and temperaments.

The octave consists of 1200 cents. A "cent" is a standard unit for measuring musical intervals. An equal-tempered semitone contains 100 cents. A "comma" is about 1/9 of an equal-tempered whole tone, or 22 cents.

Superparticular

Ratios	*Interval*	*Cents*
2:1	Octave	1200
3:2	Perfect Fifth	701.95
4:3	Perfect Fourth	498.05
	Tempered Fourths (arranged from widest to narrowest)	
	19-part scale	505.26
	1/4 comma meantone	503.42 (pure plus 1/4 comma)
	31-part scale	503.23
	43-part scale	502.33
	1/5-comma meantone	502.35 (pure plus 1/5 comma)
	equal temperament	500
	53-part scale	498.11
	Pythagorean scale	498.05 (pure)
5:4	Just Major Third	386.31

Tempered Major Thirds
(arranged from widest to narrowest)

	19-part scale	378.95
	1/4-comma meantone	386 (pure)
	31-part scale	387
	43-part scale	390.7
	1/5-comma meantone	390.61 (pure plus 1/5 comma)
	equal temperament	400
	53-part scale	497.55
	Pythagorean scale	497.83
6:5	Just Minor Third	316.64

Tempered Minor Thirds
(arranged from widest to narrowest)

19-part scale	315.79
1/4-comma meantone	310.26 (pure minus 1/4 comma)
31-part scale	309.68
43-part scale	306.98
1/5-comma meantone	307.04 (pure minus 2/5 comma)
equal temperament	300
53-part scale	294.34
Pythagorean scale	294.13

Superparticular Ratios	Interval	Cents
*7:6	Minor Third (according to Ptolemy)	266.87
8:7	Maximum tone (another interval in Ptolemy's just tuning system)	231.17
9:8	Just Whole Tone	203.91

*see page 100.

Tempered Whole Tones
(arranged from widest to narrowest)

Pythagorean scale	203.91 (pure)
53-part scale	203.77
equal temperament	200
1/5-comma meantone	195.31
43-part scale	195.35
31-part scale	193.55
1/4-comma meantone	193.16 (just major third divided in half)
19-part scale	189.47
16:15 Just Diatonic Semitone	111.73

*sotto voce: Intervals smaller than a minor third are dif-
ficult to designate by name, because there are so many
"correct" ones available. The superparticular ratio system will continue to generate intervals, which make a
continuum from whole tone, through semitone, to quar-
tertone, and finally to the commas, which are what
make a tempered interval "tempered." Some temperaments made use of two different sizes of "whole tone,"
while others used more than one size of "semitone."
Not all of these whole tones and semitones used superparticular ratios (one version of Pythagorean tuning
sported a semitone with a ratio of 256/243). It was in
part to resolve the conflict caused by too many whole
tone and semitone possibilities that Equal Temperament
was brought into being. The 19, 31, 43, and 53-part
scales listed above are also "equal temperaments" in
that their whole tone and semitone intervals are aurally
(harmonically) equal.

Suggested Reading

Leone Battista Alberti, TEN BOOKS ON ARCHITEC-
TURE, (first published in Latin in 1485). Tr. into Italian
by Cosimo Bartoli and into English by James Leoni
(1755). Alec Tiranti Ltd., London, 1955.

J. Murray Barbour, TUNING AND TEMPERAMENT: A
HISTORICAL SURVEY. Michigan State College Press,
East Lansing, 1951.

Arthur H. Benade, FUNDAMENTALS OF MUSICAL
ACOUSTICS. Oxford Univ. Press, N.Y., 1976.

Deryck Cooke, THE LANGUAGE OF MUSIC. Oxford
Univ. Press, N.Y. 1959.

Alexander J. Ellis, THE HISTORY OF MUSICAL
PITCH. Frits A.M. Knuf, Amsterdam, 1963. (Reprint of
a paper read before the Society of Arts, London, March
3,1880.)

Hermann L.F. Helmholtz, ON THE SENSATIONS OF
TONE. Dover Publications, Inc., N.Y., 1954.

Owen Jorgensen, TUNING THE HISTORICAL TEM-
PERAMENTS BY EAR. The Northern Michigan Univ.
Press, Marquette, Mich., 1977.

Sir James Jeans, SCIENCE AND MUSIC. Cambridge
Univ. Press, 1953.

Tom Keynton, HOMEMADE MUSICAL INSTRU-
MENTS. Drake Publishers, Inc., N.Y., 1975.

Douglas Leedy, "A Personal View of Meantone Temperament," THE COURANTE' (Aug. 1, 1983), p. 3.

Douglas Leedy, "In Praise of Other Intervals," CUM NOTIS VARIORUM, Jan/Feb., 1982, 7-10.

Sigmund Levarie and Ernst Levy, TONE: A STUDY IN MUSICAL ACOUSTICS. Kent State University Press, 1968.

Mark Lindley, "Interval," and "Temperaments," articles in THE NEW GROVE DICTIONARY OF MUSIC AND MUSICIANS, Stanley Sadie, Ed. MacMillan Publishers, London, 1980.

Li. S. Lloyd and Hugh Boyle, INTERVALS, SCALES, AND TEMPERAMENTS. Macdonald & Co., Ltd., London, 1963.

Ernest McClain, THE MYTH OF INVARIANCE. Nicolas Hays, Ltd., New York, 1976.

Marin Mersenne, HARMONIE UNIVERSELLE: THE BOOKS ON INSTRUMENTS. Tr. by Roger E. Chapman. Martinus Nijhoff, The Hague, Netherlands, 1956. (Orig. published 1635).

Kathi Meyer-Baer, MUSIC OF THE SPHERES AND THE DANCE OF DEATH. Princeton Univ. Press, Princeton, N.J. 1970.

Harry Partch, GENESIS OF A MUSIC. Da Capo Press, New York, 1974.

Clare Rayner, "Historically Justified Keyboard Variations on Equal Tempered Tuning," GALPIN SOCIETY JOURNAL, XXVII, April 1975, 121.

Clare Rayner, "The Wesley Kuhnle Repository at California State University, Long Beach," NOTES, XXXIII: 1, Sept., 1976, 16.

Arthur A. Reblitz, PIANO SERVICING, TUNING AND REBUILDING. The Vestal Press, Vestal, N.Y. 1976.

R. Murray Schafer, THE TUNING OF THE WORLD. Alfred A. Knopf, N.Y., 1977.

William B. White, PIANO TUNING AND ALLIED ARTS. Tuners Supply Co., Boston, 1946.

Index